MONSTER HUNTERS

FINDING SEA MONSTERS

By Bert Wilberforce

Gareth Stevens PUBLISHING

Please visit our website, www.garethstevens.com. For a free color catalog of all our high-quality books, call toll free 1-800-542-2595 or fax 1-877-542-2596.

Library of Congress Cataloging-in-Publication Data
Names: Wilberforce, Bert, author.
Title: Finding sea monsters / Bert Wilberforce.
Description: Buffalo, New York : Gareth Stevens Publishing, [2026] | Series: Monster hunters | Includes index.
Identifiers: LCCN 2024051201 (print) | LCCN 2024051202 (ebook) | ISBN 9781482472141 (library binding) | ISBN 9781482472134 (paperback) | ISBN 9781482472158 (ebook)
Subjects: LCSH: Sea monsters–Juvenile literature. | Map reading–Juvenile literature.
Classification: LCC GR910 .W55 2026 (print) | LCC GR910 (ebook) | DDC 398/.322–dc23/eng/20241206
LC record available at https://lccn.loc.gov/2024051201
LC ebook record available at https://lccn.loc.gov/2024051202

Published in 2026 by
Gareth Stevens Publishing
2544 Clinton Street
Buffalo, NY 14224

Designer: Andrea Davison-Bartolotta
Editor: Therese Shea

Photo credits: Cover, pp. 1 (sea monster), 5 (illustration), 20-21 (background) Shutterstock AI/Shutterstock.com; cover, p. 1, series art (glowing compass rose) LoveDesignShop/Shutterstock.com; series art (cardinal compass rose) Angela Ksen/Shutterstock.com; series art (fact box rope border) LanaN/Shutterstock.com; series art (fact box wood) EE SPACE/Shutterstock.com; series art (map background) Olha Andreichyn/Shutterstock.com; series art (curled paper background) MIGUEL G. SAAVEDRA/Shutterstock.com; series art (flat paper) Paladin12/Shutterstock.com; p. 5 (main) Me dia/Shutterstock.com; p. 7 File:Le Poulpe Colossal.jpg/Wikimedia Commons; pp. 7 (main), 11 (zoomed in map), 15 (map), 21 (map), 25 (map) Peter Hermes Furian/Shutterstock.com; p. 9 (inset) File:20000 squid holding sailor.jpg/Wikimedia Commons; p. 9 (main) File:Giant octopus attacks ship.jpg/Wikimedia Commons; p. 11 (bottom) chrisdorney/Shutterstock.com; p. 11 (main map) holly_molly/Shutterstock.com; p. 12 Dotted Yeti/Shutterstock.com; p. 13 Pictorial Press Ltd/Alamy Stock Photo; p. 14 Stock photos/Shutterstock.com; p. 15 (bottom) Marco Barone/Shutterstock.com; p. 16 (illustration) ZU_09/iStockphoto.com; p. 16 (background) MIGUEL G. SAAVEDRA/Shutterstock.com; p. 17 omersukrugoksu/iStockphoto.com; p. 19 (inset) File:1817 Gloucester sea serpent.jpg/Wikimedia Commons; p. 19 (main) File:Destruction of Leviathan.png/Shutterstock.com; p. 19 (frame) Tamisclao/Shutterstock.com; p. 19 (tail) ELENA SABITOVA/Shutterstock.com; p. 21 (inset) File:Kii Kuronyudo.jpg/Wikimedia Commons; p. 22 File:Kuwana - The sailor Tokuso and the sea monster.jpg/Wikimedia Commons; p. 23 F.F.YSTW/Shutterstock.com; p. 25 (inset) File:Giant Oarfish.jpg/Wikimedia Commons; p. 27 (background) Osman Temizel/Shutterstock.com; p. 27 (main) RobinGoodfellow_(m)/Flickr.com; p. 27 (squid illustration) Arip Apandi/Shutterstock.com; pp. 28, 29 (map) Janos Levente/Shutterstock.com; pp. 28, 29 (paper) AKaiser/Shutterstock.com.

Printed in the United States of America

CPSIA compliance information: Batch #CSGS26: For further information contact Gareth Stevens at 1-800-542-2595.

CONTENTS

Words in the glossary appear in **bold** type the first time they are used in the text.

SEA MONSTER HUNT

People have **explored** only about 5 percent of Earth's oceans. That might be surprising, but the oceans are huge! Oceans and seas cover nearly three-fourths of Earth. And some parts are super deep. The Mariana **Trench** in the Pacific Ocean holds the deepest point. It goes down about 36,000 feet (10,973 m)!

Years ago, the oceans were even less explored. People feared giant sea monsters hid in the water. Were they real? With the help of maps and long-told tales, you'll try to find out!

Some think sea monster tales come from people's fear of the unknown. And there's so much we don't know about what's in the oceans!

Behind the Myth

Long ago, cartographers, or mapmakers, put sea monsters on their maps. Some of these creatures were based on real animals!

THE CREEPY KRAKEN

Let's start the search with tales of the kraken. These stories from Scandinavia are more than 800 years old. Scandinavia is an area of northern Europe. It usually includes the countries of Norway, Sweden, and Denmark. People sometimes include Finland, Iceland, and the Faroe Islands too. Locate these places on the map. Many Scandinavians, including the Vikings, were fishermen and explorers of the oceans and seas.

The Norwegian Sea lies between Iceland and Norway. That's your first stop. That's where Scandinavian **myths** say the kraken lived!

A map's compass rose tells you directions on the map. For example, the Scandinavian **peninsula** (Norway and Sweden) is east of the Norwegian Sea. North (N), south (S), west (W), and east (E) are called the cardinal directions.

Behind the Myth

The British poet Alfred, Lord Tennyson, wrote a poem called "The Kraken." He **published** it in 1830. He wrote of a dangerous sea creature sleeping in deep waters.

Many Scandinavian myths say the kraken was like a large octopus or squid. How large? Some say it measured 1.5 miles (2.4 km) around! Its arms or **tentacles** were very, very long too.

Some tales said the kraken was more interested in eating fish than sailors. They said it was dangerous because it made huge waves when it came up, tipping ships over. And when the kraken sank under the water, it created a **whirlpool** that sucked ships under! But other tales said the kraken attacked ships.

Behind the Myth

Myths such as the kraken may have helped people understand hard-to-explain events, such as ships washing up on shore in pieces or disappearing forever.

Sailors and fishermen told stories of the kraken, spreading tales of the sea monster around Scandinavia and other places they visited.

A sea creature like the kraken appears in the famous Jules Verne book *Twenty Thousand Leagues Under the Seas*, published in 1869 and 1870.

THE LOCH NESS MONSTER

Head south from the Norwegian Sea to hit Scotland. No monster hunt is complete without a visit to Loch Ness. You'll find this large loch, or lake, in the Highlands, which are a rocky, hilly part of northern Scotland.

Loch Ness holds the largest **volume** of fresh water in the United Kingdom. Could it also hold a monster sometimes called Nessie? Many people think so! Tales of the Loch Ness monster have been passed down for more than 1,000 years.

Behind the Myth

An ancient people of Scotland called the Picts carved, or cut, a picture of a strange beast with flippers into stone about 1,500 years ago. Some think this was the Loch Ness monster.

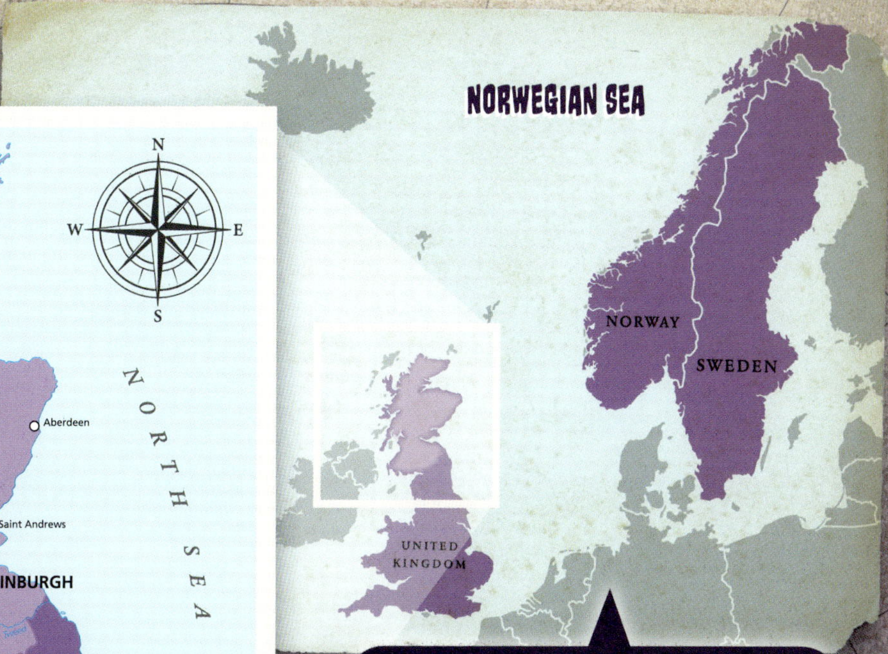

Scotland is part of the United Kingdom, a country which also includes England, Wales, and Northern Ireland.

In the 1930s, a road was paved along Loch Ness for the first time. Two people reported seeing a large creature in the water soon after. Then, in 1933, a hunter named Marmaduke Wetherell found large footprints near the water. Scientists later said they had been made with a stuffed hippopotamus foot!

Some think the Loch Ness monster is a plesiosaur, an animal that died out more than 65 million years ago. They think it hides in the loch's caves and tunnels.

In 1934, British doctor Robert Kenneth Wilson took a photo of a loch creature. For years, many believed it was real, but it was fake too. Still, scientists and others keep looking for evidence, or proof.

BEHIND THE MYTH

More than 4,000 people have reported seeing "something" in the water of Loch Ness. Many eels live in the loch. Are these what they're seeing?

The monster in Wilson's photo was made using a model and a toy **submarine.** No one knew this until 1994, though!

SCYLLA AND CHARYBDIS

The Greek **epic** called the *Odyssey* was written around 725 to 675 BCE. In it, a hero named Odysseus travels for 10 years, trying to get home. On one adventure, he must sail his ship through a narrow body of water, which is home to two terrible monsters: Scylla (SIH-lah) and Charybdis (kah-RIHB-dis).

Some think the body of water in the story is the **Strait** of Messina. It's between mainland Italy and the island of Sicily in southern Europe. Let's go!

To get to the Strait of Messina from Loch Ness, you'll travel east and then south. Use the compass rose to get there.

Rocks on one side of the Strait of Messina, shown here, were said to be the place where Scylla rested before attacking ships.

Scylla was said to have six heads with sharklike teeth on top of long snakelike necks. She had 12 feet and many dog heads around her body too. Some think Scylla represented, or stood for, a rock or **reef** that ships ran into in the strait.

In the story, Odysseus escaped these two creatures, but six of his men and his ship didn't!

Charybdis was a different kind of monster. She sucked in the waters of the strait and blew them out again several times a day. Some think Charybdis represented a dangerous whirlpool.

The Strait of Messina is about 20 miles (32 km) long. It's only 2 miles (3.2 km) wide at one point. It connects the Tyrrhenian and Ionian Seas.

Behind the Myth

The saying "between Scylla and Charybdis" means being caught between two bad choices.

SO MANY SEA SERPENTS

Sea serpents are often described as huge water snakes. Some were said to have more than one head. Tales of sea serpents go back thousands of years to the Bible and even before.

Serpents have been reported more recently too. In 1817, several people claimed to have seen a long serpent with a huge head and thick body near Gloucester Harbor, Massachusetts. In 1893, the crew of the ship *Umfuli* said they saw a large, long serpent near the Canary Islands off the northwestern African coast. They watched it for about a half hour.

In Jewish myths, God defeated, or beat, a sea serpent called the Leviathan.

Behind the Myth

The captain of the *Umfuli* said he wished "that anybody else had seen that sea-monster rather than me." Many made fun of his story and didn't believe him.

A DANGEROUS SHADOW IN JAPAN

Tentacles and snakelike bodies are scary, but is the Japanese sea monster *umi bōzu* (oo-MEE BOO-zoo) scarier? This mythical creature is described as at least as large as a ship—and sometimes much larger. It's said to be shaped somewhat like a person, but also like a dark shadow with big eyes. In some stories, the umi bōzu appears as just a head in the water!

Head to Asia to find this monster. It's said to live in the Inland Sea (Setonaikai) of Japan.

The Inland Sea is between the Japanese islands of Honshu, Shikoku, and Kyushu. This small body of water has hundreds of islands.

The umi bōzu is said to appear when the seas are calm. It makes huge waves when it comes up. It may decide to destroy a ship with one blow, take it apart piece by piece, or flood it.

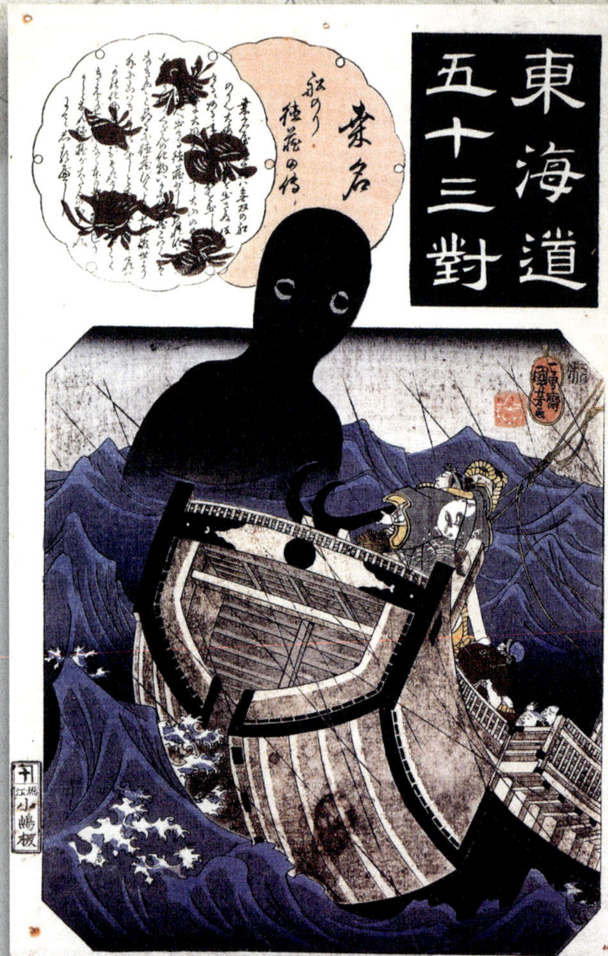

Unlike in other sea monster tales, there's a clever way to escape the umi bōzu. If the monster asks sailors for a barrel, or container, to help it flood the ship, the sailors are supposed to give it a barrel with no bottom so the water runs through it.

Behind the Myth

Some think the umi bōzu tales may come from rogue wave sightings. These are single-storm waves that seem to rise up by themselves. They happen in real life!

The Inland Sea is often calm, so tales of the umi bōzu may have tried to explain why some ships never came home.

NOT ALL JUST TALES

Many people have real-life explanations for sea monster tales and sightings. They say people could be seeing **porpoises** swimming in a line. That could look like a large sea creature's arm. Huge masses of seaweed could look like something monstrous too.

One creature might be one of the best explanations for sea monster myths. However, people didn't have evidence of this creature—the giant squid—for many years. In 2012, scientists finally got an adult giant squid on video in its habitat for the first time, near Chichi Island in the North Pacific Ocean.

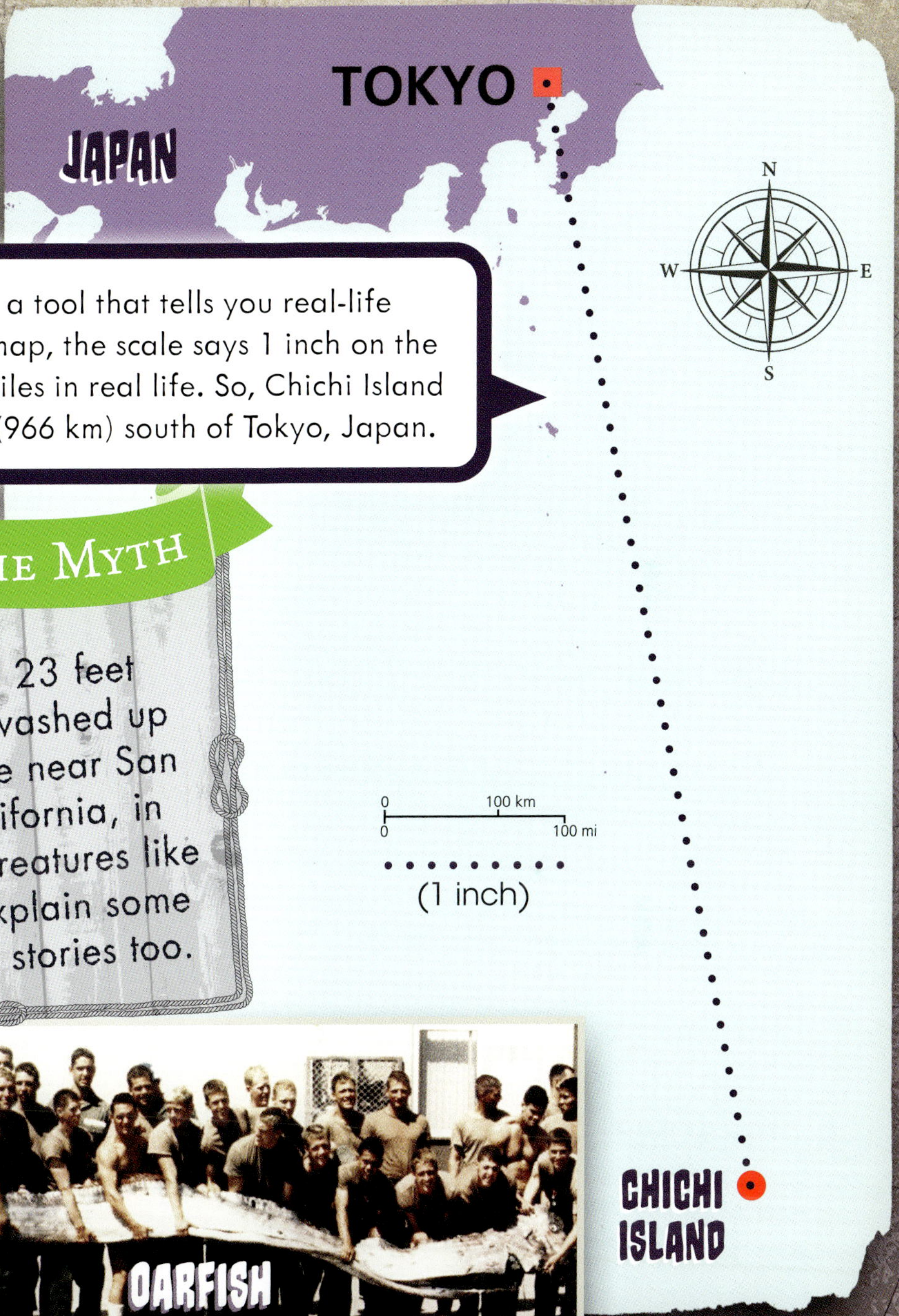

A map's scale is a tool that tells you real-life distances. On this map, the scale says 1 inch on the map is about 100 miles in real life. So, Chichi Island is about 600 miles (966 km) south of Tokyo, Japan.

Behind the Myth

An oarfish 23 feet (7 m) long washed up on the shore near San Diego, California, in 1996. Sea creatures like this could explain some sea monster stories too.

Adult giant squids can grow to be longer than 43 feet (13.1 m)! That's about as long as a school bus. There is lots of evidence that some kinds of whales attack and eat them.

Giant squids may even attack ships, likely by accident. In 1978, the USS *Stein* came head-to-head with a giant squid in the Pacific Ocean. The creature left behind teeth on the ship's body.

No matter where you go, if there's water, there's likely sea monster myths too. Keep watching the water!

Behind the Myth

The colossal squid is another huge sea creature. It can be just as large or larger than the giant squid. It also has the largest eyes of any animal—about 10 inches (25 cm) across!

This model of a sperm whale and giant squid is at the American Museum of Natural History in New York City. A battle between the two would be frightening for anyone to see.

MONSTERS IN THE WATER!

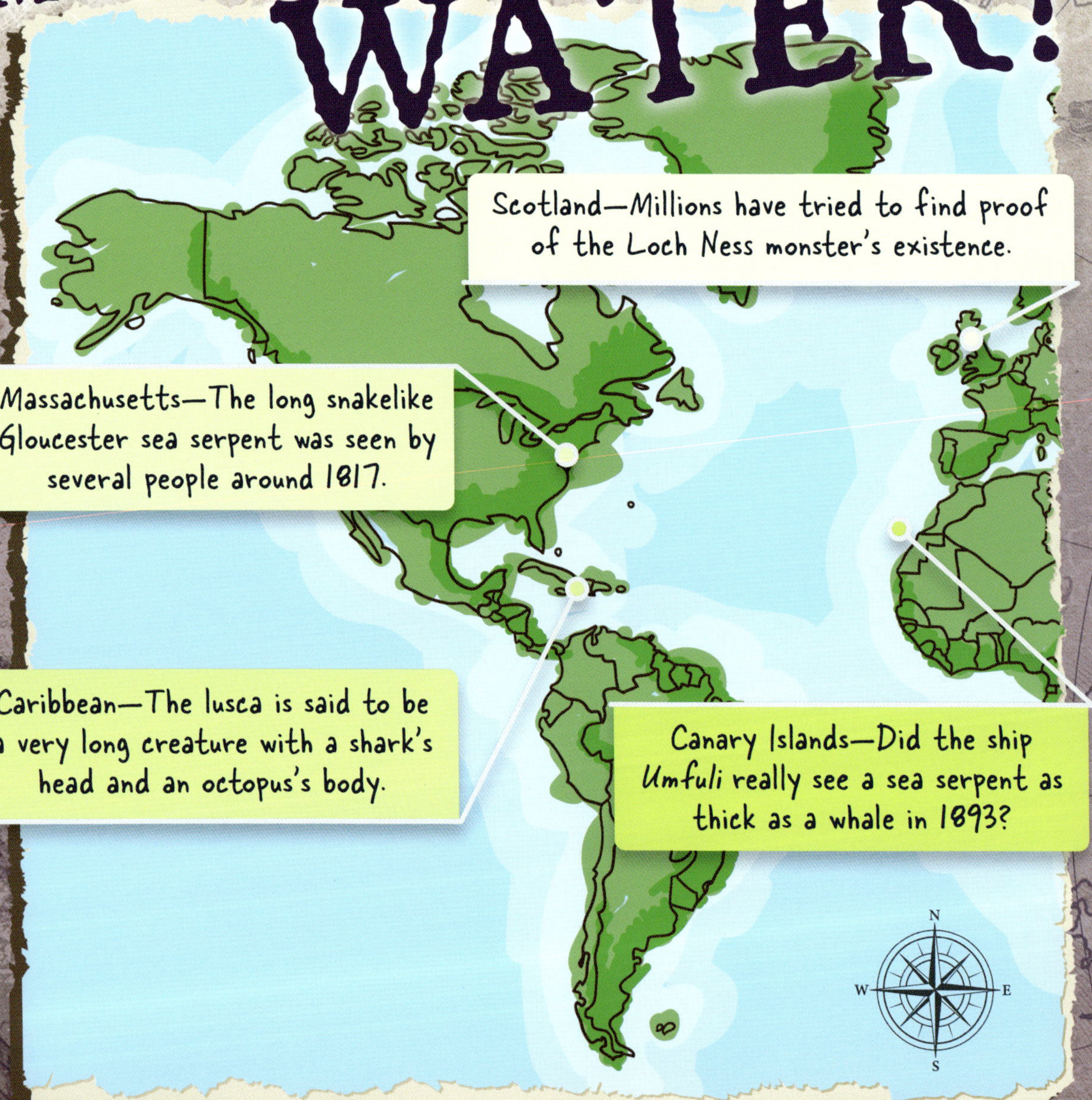

Scotland—Millions have tried to find proof of the Loch Ness monster's existence.

Massachusetts—The long snakelike Gloucester sea serpent was seen by several people around 1817.

Caribbean—The lusca is said to be a very long creature with a shark's head and an octopus's body.

Canary Islands—Did the ship *Umfuli* really see a sea serpent as thick as a whale in 1893?

Whether in fresh water or salt water, people around the world love telling tales of monsters of the deep!

GLOSSARY

epic: A long poem that tells the story of a hero's adventures.

explore: To search in order to find out new things.

myth: A story that was told by a people to explain a practice, belief, or natural event.

peninsula: A narrow piece of land that extends into water from the mainland.

porpoise: A toothed sea mammal that has a rounded nose and a triangular fin.

publish: To make a book, magazine, or other written content for people to read.

reef: A chain of rocks or coral, or a ridge of sand, at or near the water's surface.

strait: A narrow passage of water that links two large bodies of water.

submarine: A machine that can carry people or things under the water.

tentacle: A long, thin body part that sticks out from an animal's head or mouth.

trench: A long, narrow hole in the ground.

volume: A measurement of liquid that shows the amount of space it takes up.

whirlpool: Water moving quickly in a circle path that can draw objects into its center.

FOR MORE INFORMATION

Books

Drimmer, Stephanie Warren. *Prehistoric Sea Monsters.* Washington, D.C.: National Geographic, 2024.

Gleason, Carrie. *Guide to Sea Monsters.* New York, NY: Crabtree Publishing Company, 2023.

Websites

American Museum of Natural History: Sea Monsters
www.amnh.org/exhibitions/mythic-creatures/water/sea-monsters
Find out what the American Museum of Natural History says about sea monsters.

National Museum of Natural History: Sea Monsters Unearthed
naturalhistory.si.edu/exhibits/sea-monsters-unearthed-life-angolas-ancient-seas
Read about a real-life sea monster that is now extinct.

Publisher's note to educators and parents: Our editors have carefully reviewed these websites to ensure that they are suitable for students. Many websites change frequently, however, and we cannot guarantee that a site's future contents will continue to meet our high standards of quality and educational value. Be advised that students should be closely supervised whenever they access the internet.

INDEX